Rebecca Gilman

the glory of living

Rebecca Gilman is the recipient of the Roger L. Stevens Award from the Kennedy Center Fund for New American Plays and a Jeff Award for new work, both for *Spinning into Butter*, which premiered at the Goodman Theatre and received its New York premiere at Lincoln Center Theater. *The Glory of Living* premiered at the Circle Theatre in Forest Park, Illinois, and went on to receive a Jeff Citation, an *After Dark* Award, and the American Theatre Critics Association's Osborn Award. *The Glory of Living* was produced in London at the Royal Court and subsequently received the George Devine Award and the *Evening Standard* Award for Most Promising Playwright. It had its New York premiere at MCC Theater in October 2001. Ms. Gilman is also the recipient of a Guggenheim Fellowship, the Scott McPherson Award, and an Illinois Arts Council playwriting fellowship. Her other plays include *Boy Gets Girl*, which premiered at the Goodman Theatre and was named Best Play of the Year by *Time* magazine; *The Crime of the Century*; and, most recently, *Blue Surge*, which premiered at the Goodman Theatre in July 2001 and for which she received the Prince Prize for Commissioning Original Work.

the glory of
living

a play by
Rebecca Gilman

Faber and Faber
New York / London

FABER AND FABER, INC.
An affiliate of Farrar, Straus and Giroux
19 Union Square West, New York 10003

First published in 1999
by Faber and Faber Limited
3 Queen Square, London WC1N 3AU

Library of Congress Cataloging-in-Publication Data
Gilman, Rebecca Claire.
The glory of living : a play / Rebecca Gilman.—1st
American ed.
    p.   cm.
ISBN 0-571-19998-4 (pbk. : alk. paper)
    1. Children of prostitutes—Drama.   2. Runaway
teenagers—Drama.   3. Southern States—Drama.   4. Teenage
girls—Drama.   5. Murder—Drama.   I. Title.

PS3557.I456 G58 2001
812'.54—dc21

                                            2001042898

To Charles

the glory of living

The Glory of Living was first performed in the United Kingdom at The Royal Court Theatre Upstairs, West Street, London, on January 14, 1999. The cast was as follows:

Lisa   Monica Dolan
Clint   Tony Curran
Carl   Lorcan Cranitch
Carol   Joanna Griffiths
Policeman One / Hugh / Guard   Colin Mace
Girl   Milly Gregory
Angie / Jeanette / Transcriber   Linda Henry
Steve   Thomas Fisher
Jim / Policeman Two / Burrows   William Marsh

Director   Kathryn Hunter
Designer   Liz Cooke
Lighting Designer   Paule Constable
Composer   Stephen Warbeck
Sound Designer   Paul Arditti
Assistant Director   Jan Willem van der Bosch
Production Manager   Paul Handley
Company Stage Manager   Cath Binks
Stage Managers   Sara Crosdale and Kirsteen O'Kane
Costume Supervisor   Hattie Barsby
Set Construction   Rupert Blakely and Skriley's Angles

The Glory of Living presented its New York premiere at MCC Theater on October 30, 2001. Executive Artistic Directors: Robert LuPone and Bernard Telsey; Associate Artistic Director: William Cantler. The cast was as follows:

Lisa   Anna Paquin
Clint   Jeffery Donovan
Carl   David Aaron Baker
Carol   Alicia Van Couvering
Policeman Two / Hugh / Guard   Larry Clarke
Girl   Brittany Slattery
Angie   Jenna Lamia
Steve   Andrew McGinn
Jeanette / Transcriber   Erika Rolfsrud
Jim / Policeman One / Burrows   Myk Watford

Director   Philip Seymour Hoffman
Scenic Designer   Michelle Malavet
Costume Designer   Mimi O'Donnell
Lighting Designer   Jim Vermeulen
Sound Designer   David Van Tieghem
Fight Director   Rick Sordelet
Dialect Coach   Kate Wilson
Production Stage Manager   Stacy P. Hughes
Production Manager   Lester P. Grant
Press Representative   Erin Dunn Public Relations
Casting   Bernard Telsey Casting

Characters

Lisa, late teens
Clint, early thirties
Jeanette / Transcriber, late thirties
Jim / Policeman Two / Burrows, early thirties
Carol, early twenties
Girl, early teens
Angie, early twenties
Hugh / Policeman One / Guard, mid thirties
Steve, early twenties
Carl, mid to late thirties

The time is the present.

The place is various locations in Tennessee, Georgia and Alabama.

All persons and events depicted in this story are fictitious. Any resemblance to real events or persons is strictly coincidental.

Act One

SCENE ONE

At rise: the interior of a small mobile home somewhere in Tennessee. About all that can be seen is a beat-up old sofa, a table of sorts and a TV. The rest of the trailer is blocked up by a big print sheet hanging from a rope strung from the walls. While the stage itself is minimally furnished, what is there suggests poverty and disregard.

   Lisa, a girl of fifteen, enters, followed by Clint Needham and Jim Watkins, both men in their late twenties.

   Lisa is a tall girl, strong and slim with long, kind of ratty hair. She wears cut-offs and a t-shirt with some slogan on it. She is sullen and nervous.

Jim God almighty, girl. You wadn't kiddin' when you said that road was for shit.

Lisa I didn't say. My Mama said. You want my Mama.

Jim Well, you ain't so bad. (*to Clint*) She ain't so bad.

Clint Shut up. You're insultin' the lady.

Jim Shit. Where's your Mama, gal?

Lisa She's asleep.

   She goes behind the curtain.

Get up Mama, there's a guy here.

Jim (*yells*) Where's my Indian Princess? Huh?

Clint You're actin' like a pig.

Jim Where's my gal that made me laugh?

5

Lisa (*off*) Come on Mama. It's a guy.

Jeanette (*off*) What guy?

Jim It's Whippin' Wizard honey.

Jeanette (*off, sleepily*) Oh – hey! Hang on a minute, let me go pee.

Lisa (*entering*) She's goin' to clean up.

Clint How old are you, girl?

Lisa Fifteen.

Clint You go to school?

Lisa Yeah.

Clint What grade you in?

Lisa Eighth.

Clint You make good grades?

Lisa Yeah.

Clint I went to school but I didn't make good grades. No sir. I was a trouble maker. Put a frog down a girl's dress once in third grade. Little tree frog. She liked to wet her pants.

Lisa laughs a little.

Well, actually, she liked to wet her pants a lot.

Lisa laughs a little more.

Jim Y'all got anything to drink? Y'all got any Pepsi?

Lisa We got Fanta orange but it's my sister's.

Jim Oh.

Pause.

You kind of a lanky girl ain't ya? Isn't that what they'd call you, lanky?

Lisa I don't know.

Jim What's your name?

Lisa Lisa.

Jim Lisa. See, if you was to do like your Mama and talk on the CB we could call you something like Lanky Sue, or Slim in the Saddle Sue.

Lisa My name's not Sue.

Jim Yeah, but your Mama's name ain't Indian Princess either, is it?

Lisa No.

Clint Tell her what 'Whippin' Wizard' means.

Jim Nah.

Clint Tell her.

Jim Nah. She don't care.

Clint You ought to change that damn handle, man.

Jim To what? Nightrider?

Lisa I like that.

Clint That one's mine

Jeanette (*enters in a long t-shirt and shorts, looking made-up and pitiful*) Hey there.

Jim Well hey there.

Jeanette Which one of you is the Wizard?

Jim That's me. This is my friend Clint. I brung him just 'cause he wanted to go for a ride. He ain't got but to sit out here though.

7

Jeanette (*to Clint*) I can do you too, if you want.

Clint No thanks. I'll just wait.

Jeanette (*back to Jim*) When did I talk to you?

Jim Last night.

Jeanette Well I'm glad ya came by. You want something to drink? Lisa go on and get them a beer.

Jim Thanks.

Lisa exits.

Jeanette That's my littlest girl. I got two others.

Jim Where are they?

Jeanette Off somewhere. What you boys do?

Jim Me and Clint work down in Chatanooga. At the U-Tote-Em.

Jeanette Y'all have trouble finding the place?

Jim No ma'am. Them was good directions.

Clint Clear as crystal I'd say. You got a gift of expression.

Jim We saw the CB antenna right away when we was comin' by. Y'all need ta fix that road.

Jeanette The county's got ta fix that road mister. I ain't fixin' nothin'. (*She looks at Clint.*) You can talk to my girl while you're here but you don't go tryin' to mess with her.

Clint I was just –

Jeanette I ain't sayin' that 'cause of some notion I got about protectin' her or nothin'. I'm sayin' it on account of how she went and hit a boy last month tried something with her. She's big for her age.

8

Clint Shoot, she's just a girl.

Jeanette Here, you come on back here with me, Wizard man.

Jim My real name's Jim.

Jeanette It's good to know you, Jim.

> *They go behind the sheet. From the movement it is obvious that the bed is only a few feet from the 'living room' and that the sheet is the only divider. We hear Lisa from behind the sheet as well. What follows comes from behind the sheet.*

Lisa Here's your beer mister.

Jim Thanks.

Lisa You're welcome.

Jeanette Go on now.

Lisa Mama, can I watch TV?

Jeanette Go ahead.

Lisa Is that man still out there?

Jeanette He's okay honey, he's nice. Ask him to watch TV with you.

Lisa Okay.

> *She enters.*

Here's your beer mister.

Clint You can call me Clint.

Lisa You wanna watch TV?

Clint Sure.

Lisa We only get two stations.

Clint That's okay.

Lisa (*turning on the TV*) When mama talks on the CB though, we get three. Why is that?

Clint Something to do with the reception.

Lisa Yeah, I guess.

Clint You know how a TV works?

Lisa No. I kinda do, I guess. I don't know.

Clint Here's how they do it, okay? They take the picture you're seein', and they bust it up into a kijillion pieces, and they send it out over the air waves. Then your antenna, it sorts out all the pieces, and puts 'em down inta your TV.

Lisa That is so stupid.

Clint Is not.

Lisa That ain't how it works at all.

Clint Tell me how then.

Lisa I don't know, but that ain't it.

Clint You're a smart girl, huh?

Lisa Yeah.

Clint Smart all right.

Lisa Smarter than you maybe.

Clint Oh yeah.

He leans over and kisses her hard on the cheek.

Lisa Hey! Cut that shit out!

Jeanette (*off*) What's going on out there, Lisa?

Lisa (*thinks for a second, looking at Clint, trying to decide whether she should tell on him*) Nothing.

Jeanette (*off*) Shut up then.

Lisa Okay.

Jeanette laughs and cries 'Hey!' and the sheet shakes.

Clint Your Mama always do that sorta stuff with you right in the room.

Lisa It ain't the same room.

Clint It's the same room, darlin'.

Lisa She does it but I don't care.

Jim (*off*) Oh that's nice.

Pause. Clint and Lisa stare at the TV.

That is, that's nice. Come on an' take your panties off too honey.

Lisa I really don't mind on account of it happens all the time.

Pause.

So I guess I'm kinda used to it.

Clint You ain't used to it and you ain't smart.

Lisa What's that mean?

Clint You ain't used to it. I can tell by how you got yourself all hunched up on the couch like. I study people, you know. I study body language. You ever been in prison?

Lisa No!

Clint See? Smart girl. Now in prison, there's guys that'll hate you for nothing at all. For being white or for bein' a nigger, it don't matter. They hate you is all. And them nigger boys is the worst, 'cause they stick together and you maybe do one of 'em wrong and then they're all tryin' ta kill ya. So you learn to read body language real good. 'Cause maybe this or that nigger don't care nothin' 'bout you, or maybe he's out for you. So while a nigger's comin' you're figurin' things up, whether his hands is just crossed like that, or whether he's got 'em set there to grab up a knife. You gotta figure all that out in sometimes just five seconds.

Lisa You ever get beat up?

Clint Nuh-uh honey. Not me. I learned how ta read people and I became people's friend. I smiled all the time, like I do now, ya see? I smiled. You should try it too, smilin'. You might like it.

Lisa I smile plenty.

Clint So see honey, I can see as how you're not comfortable with what your mama puts on.

Lisa So?

Clint So maybe you'd like to get the hell out of here.

Lisa I ain't going anywhere with you.

Clint Did I ask you to? No. That's where you're not so smart neither. For instance, a minute ago you didn't have no idea I was goin' to kiss you on the cheek did you?

Lisa No, 'cause only a low-down fool would do that.

Clint (*laughs*) You got me pegged, gal! That's me. A low-down fool.

Lisa You think that's funny?

Clint I do. Maybe you ain't so dumb at all.

Lisa Maybe you don't know nothin' about it.

Clint That's a fact.

Pause. As soon as they stop talking they become aware of the sounds of love-making coming from behind the curtain.

Lisa (*shyly*) How come you were in prison?

Clint Well, that's a silly story, but I stole some cars.

Lisa How many?

Clint Well, just one at a time. But I started around when I was fifteen or so.

Lisa Like me huh?

Jeanette (*off*) Ooh baby, don't touch me there, it tickles.

Jim (*off*) Okay then, here!

Jeanette shrieks.

Clint She okay?

Lisa She's all right. She's a screamer.

Clint Oh.

Pause.

So anyway, I started stealing cars when I was about fifteen. Me and my friend Matt, we'd steal some little something and take it out by my farm and drive it about a hundred miles an hour down back roads. Then we'd dump it somewhere.

Lisa Cool.

Clint Yeah. We got busted off to juvenile homes a couple of times but that didn't stop us.

Jim (*off*) Oh god, oh that's good.

Clint But then we got to our majority and they started a record, you know, repeat offender. Last time I got caught they put me up for fifteen months.

Lisa Man.

Clint Yeah, it really was a buncha nothin'. That judge, he said, 'Son, if you behave yourself, you'll be out in six months.' And I said, 'Well then judge, I'll see ya in fifteen.'

Lisa laughs. Clint smiles at her and they look at each other for a few seconds. The sounds of her mother reaching orgasm are becoming painfully clear, as her moaning does indeed turn into a louder sort of screaming.

Jim (*off*) Oh god yes, oh god yes, oh yes, oh, I'm comin'! I'm comin'! I'm comin'!

The two seem to reach orgasm together and there is a moment's heavy panting and breathing.
Pause.

Lisa She fakes it.

Clint How do you know that?

Lisa She tole me.

Clint Where's your daddy?

Lisa He died.

Jeanette (*off*) Ow!

Jim (*off*) Sorry.

Lisa He wrecked his motorcycle when I was ten.

Clint I think you're real special.

Lisa Special how?

14

Clint I kinda like the way you look.

Lisa I ain't nothin' to look at.

Clint Yes you are gal. I ain't never seen anything as pretty as you.

> *Beat*

You like me?

Lisa I like you okay.

Clint You're a good listener. You don't just pretend.

> *Beat.*

You wanta go out in my truck? Ride around?

Lisa (*considers*) Can we go down ta the quarry?

Clint You gotta show me where it is.

Lisa There's a junked up old car down there. There's like, just the seat, ya know. Just the old seat, an' some of the sides of the car, but there ain't no roof. You can sit in there.

Clint Sit in there and do what?

Lisa Lean back. Look up.

Clint You just show me where, sister.

Lisa Okay.

Clint Okay. Now you're so smart. Tell me what I'm going ta do.

Lisa I don't know.

Clint Tell me where I'm gonna kiss you.

Lisa On the mouth?

Clint See. Told you you was smart.

He kisses her. Blackout

End of scene.

SCENE TWO

At rise: the interior of a cheap motel room. The same furniture from before can be used in a different configuration. Lisa and Clint are lying in one of the beds, naked. They are arranged so that the head of the bed is stage right or left, so that the audience cannot see behind the bed. Clint is eating potato chips out of a plastic bag.

Clint We don't gotta go down there honey. I just thought, that maybe once, you could see things the way I do and support me in tryin' to get somethin' good for us.

Lisa I always support you.

Clint You do not.

Lisa I do too. I been all over this damn state supportin' you.

Clint Who does the work around here?

Lisa Nobody.

Clint Who done it before?

Lisa I could work if you let me.

Clint Uh-uh gal, you cannot. You got no diploma.

Lisa Neither do you.

Clint Uh-uh. They'll take you away from me again.
I ain't sittin' in no goddamn jail again while you go out

getting it with some goddamn nigger gettin' it on day and night with some goddamn nigger.

Lisa Hardly.

Clint Don't talk like that to me.

Lisa Hardly gettin' it on with nobody.

Clint You said.

Lisa I said nothin'. Nothin' is what I said. Hell. I couldn't a got it on with nobody. I was big as a fuckin' house.

Clint (*conceding*) That's true.

Lisa And then my cooter was all ripped up to hell and sore. Hell it was sore. And they shaved off all my hair down there and man did it itch. Shit.

Clint Aw honey. I can't believe I wasn't there for you, with you goin' through all that sufferin', and me beggin' them sons a bitches, sayin', 'Please. You just gotta let me out please. My wife is havin' a baby.'

Lisa (*quietly*) Two babies.

Clint I didn't know that then. If I'd a known that I woulda asked twice as hard. 'Please please mister, you gotta let me go, I'm gonna be a daddy.'

Lisa (*laughs*) I like the way you say that, 'I'm gonna be a daddy!' It makes you sound like a little boy.

Clint And you're my little girl.

He strokes her hair.

You are all there is, Lisa girl.

Lisa Ha!

Clint It's true.

Lisa Ha ha!

Clint I don't care if you don't believe me, it's the god's truth.

Pause.

Lisa Clint, I wanna see the twins.

Clint We'll go up to my mama's soon an' get 'em.

Lisa They're at my mama's.

Clint They ain't.

Lisa They are too.

Clint Girl, your mama's a whore. We did not leave them with your mama.

Lisa I thought we did.

Clint Girl, your mama is a drunk whore.

Lisa Yeah, so?

They laugh.

Clint Aw honey, I don't know if you can feel it, but pretty soon you and me is gonna be set. There ain't gonna be a single town that hadn't felt us comin' and goin'.

Lisa Where's your gun? I wanna see your gun.

Clint I don't wanna get up honey.

Lisa I wanta see it.

Clint I don't wanta get up honey. I'm all comfortable like I am now. Right here like I am now.

Lisa I wish you'd let me see it. I like it when you let me hold it.

Clint Hold somethin' else gal, right under here.

He lifts up the sheet.

Lisa Can you do it again?

Clint What's that s'posed ta mean? Huh?

She doesn't answer him.

Answer me, Lisa gal.

Lisa It don't mean nuthin'. It just means, I wanna do it again too. If you wanna. If you don't neither, that's okay. That's okay too.

Clint I tell you this once and you hear me good. Hear me good girl. I can do it whenever I goddamn please. You hear that? I can do it whenever I goddamn please!

Lisa Okay. I'm sorry.

Clint You fuckin –

He shoves her violently out of the bed, onto the floor.

Lisa Okay, okay, okay.

She gets up. On her naked body we can see a host of bruises. She walks quietly over to the bathroom door and goes inside.

Clint (*yelling after her*) Where're you goin'? You bitch. Go in there and wash me out. Go in there and wash me out of you. I know that's what you're doin'.

He reaches over the side of the bed, upstage from the audience, and grabs something heavy and starts to pull. It is a slight girl, around fifteen years old. She is handcuffed to the head board and she is wearing a t-shirt and panties. She seems to be unconscious but as he starts pulling on her she starts to moan.

Get up here! Come on you little chit, get up here!

He pulls her onto the bed with him, and then lies there for a second, recovering his breath from the effort.

Jesus.

Pause.

You awake?

She doesn't respond. He starts to prod her.

Hey? Girl? You awake?

He shakes her.

Wake up! I wanna talk to you. You still sick?

She groans.

You look sick.

Beat.

You prob'ly never got drunk before, huh? I bet you hadn't. We maybe shoudn'ta made you drink all that. Lisa one time gave one of the babies a drink. Made it sleep for hours. I said, 'That's good stuff.'

Pause.

'We oughta bottle that and sell it for cough medicine.'

Pause. He starts rubbing her stomach over her t-shirt.

We done lotsa stuff. Me and Lisa. Mostly me though. I robbed a Jitney Jungle once. They got those in Alabama? They got 'em in Florida. They're just like a Mini Mart, only better.

Beat.

I was gonna rob some more, maybe. But I got sent up
for a while, for kiting checks. Well, for stealing too.
From the U-Tote-Em where I worked. Took shit all the
time. (*Beat. Fondly*) Lisa usedta come to work with me.
I'd lay her down on the floor of the cooler, on that cold
cement floor, and I'd do to her what nobody else is done
to her. I'd turn her legs up and go to it. She'd say it hurt
her back, on that cement floor. I'd say, 'Good. It's
supposeta hurt. It's the best kinda hurt there is.' She
didn't really mind it. (*Beat.*) Lisa likes you cause you
was in a juvenile home too. Wadn't you?

He starts to pay a little more attention to her.

You're kinda pretty.

*He starts to pull her t-shirt up. He stops half way and
starts to rub her stomach again.*

You sick huh? My mama usedta rub my tummy like this
when I was feelin' sick. She'd give me a warm coke and
she'd rub my tummy and hum, hum, hum.

*Pause, he tenderly rubs her stomach, making small
circles with his hand. He hums tunelessly.*

'Course I don't know no songs.

He stops and looks at her.

Lisa knows this, and she knows how I hate for her to
say this out loud to me, but I sometimes can't do it more
'n one time a day, on account of how much I put out at
a time, and my resources can't build back up too fast.
'Cause of the output.

He pulls her shirt back down.
   Pause.
He looks at her. He calls.

Lisa! Come on out here, gal. I ain't mad no more.

Pause.

Come out. I'm sorry I shoved on you. I ain't mad at you.
Come out.

The bathroom door opens a crack.

Come on.

Lisa What for?

Clint Come on.

Lisa What for?

Clint You hear me don't ya?

Lisa Okay.

She comes out with a towel around her.

How come you got her up on the bed?

Clint I ain't doin' nothin' with her.

Lisa What you want me for?

Clint Come on over here and see if you can wake her
up.

Lisa She ain't hurtin' nobody.

Clint I know. Come on over here.

Lisa She's a little girl.

Clint Come on.

Lisa makes her way, haltingly, to the bed.

Lay down here between us.

She crawls between them.

Let's all get under the covers, nice and family like.

Lisa You ought to unhook her, it'd be easier.

Clint Uh-uh. I don't think so. Now here. You lie there and see if you can't wake her up. I wanna watch you try.

Lisa How?

Clint Nice like. You rub on her and you kiss on her and you see if you can't wake her up.

Lisa I don't know how.

Clint Oh yes you do baby. You know you do. Go on now. I wanna watch.

Lisa I don't know how.

Clint Oh yes you do.

Blackout.

SCENE THREE

The lights come up on the girl, still in the bed. She is awake now and sitting up, hugging her knees, with the sheet pulled up around her neck. Lisa is getting dressed. She is rooting through a duffel bag, looking for some jeans.

Lisa I just, I just can't find anything in here. It's sucha mess. Me and Clint, we ain't normally this messy you know. We just, well, we been on the road for a while now and you know . . . living in motels.

She giggles nervously

You get useta the maids an' all.

She pulls out some jeans and smells them.

(*To herself almost*) These ain't too bad I guess. Sometimes they get that cum smell on 'em . . . I mean, you know.

23

Girl I know.

Lisa You do?

Girl Yeah.

Lisa You thirsty or something?

Girl (*almost crying*) I really gotta go to the bathroom, please, I gotta go so bad.

Lisa Oh. Okay. I mean, oh. I don't know what to do.

Girl Please. I'm gonna go in my pants. I hurt so bad.

Lisa (*starts looking around aimlessly*) Okay. Okay. Okay. I'll just, I'll just unlock these things and go with you. But you gotta promise not to run away.

Girl I promise, please.

Lisa Okay. I'm gonna unlock these things. I'm a mama you know. I know how it gets bad and all.

She unlocks her

Okay. You go in here, just go in an I'll close the door. You go on.

The girl limps into the bathroom and closes the door.

Just tell me when you're through. Okay?

Girl (*off*) Okay.

Lisa (*putting on the jeans. Talking to fill the time*) After this we gotta go somewhere. It ain't far but we gotta go. I'm gonna go get my kids first. They're up at my mama's. And then we're gonna go somewhere together. Just us. I got my own car. Me an' Clint, we gotta have separate cars, on account of how he sometimes has business he gotta take care of.

Beat.

24

We talk on the CB a lot though. In our cars. He'll call me up sometimes and pretend he don't know me an' act like we're meetin' right there on the radio and arrangin' to go to some motel together. Just to keep things interestin' an' all. 'Count of how we been married so long. We been married two whole years. Come August.

Beat

You doin' okay in there?

Girl (*off*) I guess.

Lisa You ready to come out?

Girl (*opening the door*) I guess.

Lisa You gonna flush?

Girl No.

Lisa You wipe?

Girl Yeah.

Lisa Okay. Sit down over there while I get ready.

Girl Okay.

Lisa Was you in that home long before you ran away?

Girl 'Bout four months.

Lisa You glad we give you a ride?

Girl I guess.

Lisa We coulda took you to the police.

Girl I'm glad you didn't do that. They caught me once before.

Lisa What'd they do to you?

Girl Took me home.

Lisa Is that why you was in that home? 'Cause you run away all the time?

Girl Nah. They put me in there for protection.

Lisa Oh. Somebody beat on you.

Girl No. It was this man my mama lived with. He useta come in the living room and make me lie on the couch, and he'd put his fingers in me.

Lisa I'll be glad when I turn eighteen. Then they cain't put me in them homes no more. They wouldn't a done it at all, 'cept Clint was in jail. And I was pregnant.

Girl I hate it there. The food sucks.

Lisa Yeah. They don't let you sleep late neither.

Girl Yeah. I hate that.

Lisa You look like a girl from TV. Like Joanie from *Happy Days*.

Girl Well, I wish that y'all would let me go.

Lisa How come?

Girl 'Cause I'm sick. He hurt somethin' in me.

Lisa He's real big. He made my gash bigger.

Girl He's mean.

Lisa stops packing and stares at her.

Lisa He is?

Girl Yeah. Anyway, can I go now?

Lisa No. I cain't let you. I'm sorry. But it's okay. I'm takin' you out of here. I'm gonna go get my kids and then I'm takin' you out of here.

Girl You gonna give me a ride?

Lisa Yeah. Where're your pants and stuff.

Girl Under the bed.

Lisa You get 'em and get dressed. You'll feel better. I promise.

Girl Okay.

She crawls to the other side of the bed and disappears onto the floor.

Lisa I'm real sorry you're sick. None of this was my idea though. You gotta know that. Okay?

Girl Okay.

Comes back up with some pink pants.

I'm gonna put these back on.

Lisa Good girl. Just know it too though.

Girl Know what?

Lisa (*pauses*) Nothin'. Never mind.

Lisa I got just about everything.

Girl I can't find my shoes.

Lisa Clint took 'em.

Girl How come?

Lisa He's like that. But you don't worry. You won't be seein' him ever again.

Girl (*almost smiles*) Good.

Lisa (*turns off the light*) We gotta be real quiet. We ain't paid the bill. Now you just hold my hand and come on.

Girl Okay.

Lisa Be good now.

Girl Okay.

Lisa Be good.

End of scene.

SCENE FOUR

Lights up on a very similar motel room. The beds have a different spread, but the atmosphere is the same. Dirty and cheap. Again, of the two beds, only one has been slept in and again, there are soda cans, candy wrappers, etc., all around the place. Clint sits on the bed, fully dressed. A nineteen-year-old woman, Carol, sits next to him, eating from a big bag of pretzels and drinking a Pepsi. Lisa is yelling at Clint.

Lisa You can't tell me you don't like her! I drove around all goddamn day tryin' to get one. You can't tell me you don't like her! They ain't nothin' wrong with her. She's nice.

Clint It ain't that I don't like her, honey. It's just that she kinda gives me the creeps.

Lisa She's nice. Ask her somethin'. You'll see.

To Carol, yelling.

Tell him how nice you are!

Carol Y'all seem nice too.

Lisa See? See?

Clint I guess.

Lisa You ain't never satisfied with nothin' I do for you. I could grow two heads and you'd still say I wadn't smart enough. I could grow six legs.

Clint (*laughs*) You'd be a bug.

Lisa You ain't funny, not one bit funny. I been tryin' all goddamn day. All goddamn day.

Clint Okay honey. Okay. I'll talk to her.

Turns to Carol.

What's your name, honey?

Carol Carol.

Clint That's nice. This is Lisa an' I'm Clint.

Carol I know. How come y'all didn't want Steve comin' back with us?

Clint He didn't wanta come.

Carol How come y'all didn't give him a ride home? He doesn't like the woods. I don't think he wanted to stay in the woods.

Lisa Yes he did. He said so.

Clint Them pretzels good?

Carol Yeah.

Pause.

Can I have another coke?

Clint Yeah. Sure. Here's fifty cents. You can go get it.

Lisa Clint!

Clint Honey, she ain't goin' nowhere.

Lisa Clint!

Clint Go on, Carol honey.

He ushers her out the door.

Lisa, calm down.

Lisa She's gonna call the fuckin' cops!

Clint No she ain't. Can't you see? She's simple.

Lisa Simple what?

Clint Simple. Touched. She's got somethin' wrong with her.

Lisa Retarded?

Clint Could be. There was a bunch a kids in my school like that. They had a special class.

Lisa Oh.

Clint I usedta pick on them kids somethin' awful till one day, my teacher, she sat me down and said, 'Now Clint, you're a lucky boy. You're smart and you got a way with people. Them kids, they's got no luck in this world at all, and then you go and heap misery on them, they don't deserve that.' An' I seen right away how she was right. And after that, anybody went to pick on one them kids, I'd hit 'em so hard they'd shit theirselves.

Lisa Is that true?

Clint How come you question all I say?

Lisa It don't sound like you to stick up for somebody.

Clint Well I did and you better stop questionin' me 'cause it always sounds like you're mockin' me and I cain't abide that behaviour at all.

Lisa Okay.

Clint You sorry?

Lisa I'm sorry, Clint.

Carol comes back in with another Pepsi.

Carol Thanks, mister.

Clint You're welcome, honey.

Pause. He looks at Lisa while he says this.

You wanna do somethin' else for me?

Carol What's that?

Clint You wanta take off your clothes?

Carol Oh. Y'all wanna do that?

Clint Yeah, honey. We wanna do that.

Carol Okay.

She starts taking off her clothes.

Lisa (*to Clint*) Shoot. Look at her. She's ugly.

Clint She's okay.

Lisa She din't even flinch when you asked her. She don't even care about her boy-friend. Hey. Hey girl. What would your boy-friend say about this?

Carol (*with her shirt over her head*) I don't know. We never did this.

Lisa You a virgin?

Carol No. I done it lots with other guys. That's how I get rides home.

Lisa Oh. (*to Clint*) You look see she ain't got no bumps or nothin' on her. I don't want no twat rot.

Clint Where you learn that language? Your mama teach you ta talk like that? I swear.

Lisa I just don't want nothin' bad comin' of this. I feel nervous. I'm all on edge.

Clint Don't be. Go on now. Go on and go for a drive.

Lisa (*crushed*) Clint. I been in the car all day. I'm so tired. Please don't make me go. I can just lie on the other bed. I can just watch TV real quiet. Please honey.

Clint Aw sweety. You know how you get. Now go on.

Lisa No. I promise I won't. I swear. Please. You know I'm different now. You know how different I can be. Please. Don't make me go.

Clint You don't wanta stay, honey. Now go.

He gets up and starts pushing her slowly toward the door.

Lisa Please.

Clint No ma'am.

He opens the door and pushes her out.

Lisa (*near tears*) Clint . . .

Clint (*he pulls his arm back, as if to slap her. She steps back. He points his finger in her face*) You know. Don't mess with me. Here, take your purse.

He shoves it at her and closes the door, then turns to Carol.

See how she's devoted ta me? I swear I love that girl.

Carol She your daughter?

Clint Honey. That gal is my wife, thank you.

Carol (*laughs*) You're married.

Clint (*looks at her*) You wanna do this really?

Carol Sure. Lemme drink some more coke. Them pretzels make me thirsty.

Clint I bet. You know how to do it with your mouth?

Carol I know that.

Clint Well, you're a real find. Lisa done good.

Carol Will y'all give me a ride back home?

Clint Of course we will honey. Of course.

Blackout.

SCENE FIVE

The hotel room, the next day. Lisa is alone. She is on the phone, waiting nervously.

Lisa Hello? This the police station? . . . Um, no. I don't guess it's an emergency. I just got some information. It's about a girl. Up at Kentwood. State Park. Up there. There's a, there's a um . . . a missin' girl up there. She was at the Harpstead Home. She ran away from there.

Pause.

No ma'am. I don't know her name. But I seen her body up there. (*Pause. Then quickly*) No ma'am I cain't give you my name. You just, you just got to go up there, if you go up there through the main park part, up ta the parkin' lot, and then there's a lookout spot? Go up there and look down in the canyon and you'll see where they dumped her body. Down there. You'll see her if you go up there and look.

She hangs up quickly.
Pause.

33

She looks around nervously. Then she crosses to the TV and turns it on, gets on the bed and lies there, her arms by her side, waiting.
Blackout.

SCENE SIX

The same hotel room. Empty. The TV is on but that is the only light. Sounds of scuffling from outside, then Lisa and Clint enter. He is half-dragging her. They are both drunk.

Clint C'mon honey. Walk on in. You just put one foot in front of the other. Just walk like when you was a baby. Just walk.

Lisa Clint?

Clint Yeah darlin'?

Lisa I am so drunk.

She begins to laugh.

Clint Lisa?

Lisa Yeah darlin'?

Clint You are so drunk.

Lisa Shuddup!

Clint You are!

Lisa You are so mean!

Clint You are so drunk!

They collapse on the bed, giggling. Clint pulls Lisa to him and holds her.

Honey? Hey, honey?

34

Lisa Yeah?

Clint You wanna know somethin'?

Lisa What?

Clint You wanna know how much I love you?

Lisa How much?

Clint I love you so much it makes me sick sometimes.

Lisa That ain't nice.

Clint No I mean it. Sick with worryin'. Sick with bein' jealous. I get crazy jealous over you.

Lisa I know.

Clint I see a guy lookin' at you, I wanna eat him alive.

Lisa Nobody looks at me no how.

Clint Oh honey.

Lisa Uh-huh. I'm a ugly ole hag. Ugly an' old as the hills.

Clint You're a goddamn baby. My goddamn baby girl.

He strokes her hair.

Honey?

Lisa Yeah.

Clint Promise you ain't never gonna leave me.

Lisa (*beat*) You know I ain't.

Clint Promise.

Lisa I promise.

Clint Me too. I promise you too. Don't you be scared a' that.

Lisa I ain't.

Clint Sometimes, I look up at night, up at the ceilin' and I think as how all there is of me is right there. Right there floatin' between the bed an' the roof. I think I'm gonna wake up in the mornin' wishin' I hadn't. You ever feel that?

Lisa I don't think so.

Clint Look up at the ceilin' now. Tell me what it makes you think.

Lisa It makes me think the bed is spinnin'.

Clint Uh-oh. You got the spins.

Lisa Ugh.

Clint Close your eyes.

He puts his hand over her eyes.

Keep 'em closed.

Lisa I feel sick.

Clint Shhh. Shh. Keep 'em closed, honey.

Lisa Okay.

Clint You go to sleep now.

Lisa Okay.

Clint Go to sleep and I'll stay here. I'll stay here. I'll watch TV.

Lisa (*quietly*) Okay.

Clint Shhhh.

He holds his hand over her eyes. Slow fade out. End of scene.

Same hotel room. Next day. The TV is off but everything else is the same. Lisa enters, throws down her purse on the bed.

Lisa Shit.

> *She sits on the bed. Kicks at an empty can on the floor. She is like a pouty, disappointed child.*

They didn't even clean the room.

> *Sound of a car door slamming. Clint enters, in the same mood.*

They don't even clean the rooms around here. What's the deal?

Clint What'd you come back for?

Lisa I didn't wanna do it any more.

Clint What about that one girl?

Lisa She wouldn't get in the car.

Clint Why not?

Lisa I don't know why not. She almost was, I think, but then she changed her mind.

Clint What'd you say to her?

Lisa I said, 'You wanna go for a ride?' That's all.

Clint Shit.

Lisa I cain't help it.

Clint You can too.

Lisa No I cain't.

Clint We gotta get you cleaned up. I bet if you washed your hair they'd git in with you.

Lisa They don't care about my hair. They just know somethin' funny is gonna happen.

Clint What does that mean? Somethin' funny.

Lisa They just know. They're scared.

Clint 'Cause you're scared.

Lisa I don't act scared. I act normal.

Clint You don't know what normal is.

Lisa Don't be mad.

Clint I'm goin' back out. I'm gonna find me somebody myself.

Lisa Why don't you just do it with me? Just tonight.

Clint (*pause. Looks at her*) Not tonight. Honey. Naw. Not you tonight. I gotta taste for somethin' different.

Lisa I don't see why.

Clint I don't expect you to.

Lisa You could tell me.

Clint You wouldn't get it.

Looks in the mirror.

How do I look?

Lisa You look okay.

Clint Yeah, but do I look good?

Lisa You look good.

Clint How's my hair?

He reaches up and pats it.

Lisa It's kinda messy.

Clint Come over here then.

He pulls a comb out of his pocket and hands it towards her.

Gimme a comb.

He sits on the edge of the bed. She crawls up behind him and crouches on her knees. She begins combing his hair.

Get a nice clean part.

Lisa I will.

Clint Not too far over.

Lisa I know.

She finishes up. Hands him back the comb.

Here.

Clint (*pats his head again*) Okay. What about my shoes?

Without hesitation Lisa crawls down onto the floor and begins retying his shoes.
   He reaches in his pocket and pulls out some money and puts it on the bed.

Here. In case you want a coke or somethin'.

Lisa Thanks.

Clint Don't be mad.

Lisa I ain't mad.

Clint Don't be.

Lisa I ain't.

She finishes and sits back.

Clint I'll be back in a while. You go on an' wash your hair. Try not to look so scary.

Lisa Okay.

Clint See ya.

He exits.
Long pause. Lisa gets up, walks over to the window and looks through the curtains. When she is certain he is gone she goes to the phone and dials.

Lisa Hey. Is this the police? Yeah. I called a while back, about a missin' girl, about her bein' up at the state park. Remember? Well, I gotta talk fast, but I know where there's a girl and a boy that's missin'. They're, if you go down, go down by Huntsville, down south a' Huntsville there's a road called Turkey Creek Road. Run down that road a ways and there's like a Golden Gallons, an' a tire place. And then there's some big electric plant. Go past that plant and there's a road that turns off to the left, just past Route 35, and goes up over some railroad tracks. Go back on that road a ways to where you see a creek, and past that, a little hollow place. And look there. That's where they are. Back in there.

She hangs up. The phone rings immediately. She screams. Then she picks it up nervously, doesn't say anything for a second.

Hello?

Beat.

No ma'am. No ma'am, the room hadn't been cleaned. Yeah. I'd 'preciate that. Bye.

She hangs up and stares at the phone. Blackout.
End of scene.

SCENE EIGHT

Clint, Lisa, and Angie are seated on the ends of the bed, watching TV. They all seem uncomfortable.

Angie Y'all don't have to watch this. If you want to watch somethin' else. I don't care.

Lisa This is okay. I'm sorry about how the room looks. They called down here and said they was gonna clean it, but nobody ever came.

Angie I don't care.

Clint What do y'all wanta do?

Angie I think I gotta go.

Clint You just got here.

Angie I know. But I gotta go. It's late.

Clint It ain't late.

Angie Yeah. It is.

Clint I thought you wanted to ride around some.

Angie We already did. It got kinda boring.

Clint Well, let's just watch some TV.

Angie (*sighs*) Okay.

Clint Lisa could go get some beer.

Lisa I'll get carded.

Clint We can all go.

Angie Nah. If you're gonna go I'd just as soon go home.

Clint I think you oughta stay.

Pause.

Maybe you'd have more fun if we fooled around some.

Angie What?

Clint You know?

Angie You me and her?

Clint Or just you and me. She can go out somewhere.

Angie No way!

Clint What's wrong?

Angie Nothin'. I just ain't foolin' around with you is all.

She gets up.

Clint Where're you goin'?

Angie Home.

Clint (*rises*) No ma'am.

Angie What's your problem?

She moves toward the door. He crosses to her quickly, grabbing her by the arm.

Let go!

Clint No ma'am. I spent all day lookin' for you. Come on back here.

Angie Let me go!

She struggles. Clint pushes her on the bed, on top of Lisa.

Lisa Ouch!

Clint Get out of the way!

He shoves Lisa on the floor.

Lisa Stop it!

She gets up.

She said she don't want to!

*Clint backhands her across the face. She loses her
balance and falls again. Angie has gotten up and is
headed for the door. Clint grabs her by the belt and
pulls her back. She slaps him and he shoves her on the
bed again. He gets on top of her and puts his hand
over her mouth.*

Clint Calm down.

*Lisa gets up slowly and looks at them. She moves
towards the bathroom. Clint ignores her.*

Just lemme git these jeans off.

*He reaches down to unzip Angie's jeans. She hits him
hard on the nose.*

Fuck!

*He grabs at his nose and sits back. Angie pushes him
and squirms out from under him. She rushes to the
door.*

Stay there you goddamn cunt!

*He lunges at her. Angie gets the door open and
standing there are two policemen. They all stare at
each other for a moment.*

Policeman One Ma'am?

Angie What?

Policeman One Are you Lisa Needham, ma'am?

Angie Help me.

Policeman One Are you Lisa Needham, ma'am?

Angie No. I'm not. Help me.

Policeman Two Who are you, sir?

Clint (*still holding his nose, talking through his hand*) My name's Clint Needham.

Policeman Two (*to Angie*) Is he any relation to you?

Angie He was tryin' to kill me.

Policeman One Is that true, sir?

Clint No. No. We was just . . . she was . . . we was just foolin' around. We ain't done nothin'.

Policeman One What happened to your nose, sir?

Clint Nothin'. I got a cold.

Angie I hit him. He was shovin' me on the bed. He was gonna kill me.

   Beat. The policemen stare at her.

Help me.

Policeman One Okay ma'am. We'll help you. Sir? Could you just move slowly back into the room and turn to the wall? Could you just put your face to the wall and your hands behind your head, with your fingers interlocking?

   Clint starts to move.

Clint My nose is busted. Are you gonna do anything about my busted nose?

   He moves into the room as instructed.

Policeman Two (*seeing Lisa in the back*) Are you Miz Needham ma'am?

Lisa Yeah.

   Beat.

Is this somethin' about my babies?

Policeman One No ma'am. This is something else.
I wonder if you and Mr Needham and this young
lady would consent to come down to the police station
with us?

Clint What for?

Policeman Two To answer some questions.

Clint 'Bout what?

Policeman Two About some murders.

Clint (*turns back from the wall*) No. We won't.

Policeman One Then we'll have to place you and Miz
Needham under arrest, sir.

Clint Under arrest?

Policeman One Yessir.

Clint (*turned to the police, with his hands still behind
his head*) Y'all are the goddamn end. You know that?
Where'd you learn ta talk like that? Police school?

Policeman One (*not understanding*) I'm sorry sir?

Clint That's it. You call me 'sir' one more time an' I'm
gonna have to rip your fuckin' face off. You unnerstand?

*He pulls his hands down. Neither of the policemen
react, except to stare at him. Long pause.*

Policeman One Yes. Yes I do.

Small beat.

Sir.

*Lights fade out.
End of Act One.*

Act Two

SCENE ONE

At rise: a police station interrogation room. There is a table and a couple of chairs. A tape recorder sits on the table. Lisa sits in one of the chairs. She looks around nervously. She is clutching a red, plastic, toy piano, about the size of a lunchbox. One of the legs of the piano is broken. She stares off into space and then instantly is alert when a detective, Bob Burrows, enters. He is a youngish, heavy-set man in a suit.

Burrows (*pauses for a moment, looks at Lisa*) Miss Needham?

Lisa Mrs Needham.

Burrows Mrs Needham. My name is Bob Burrows. I'm a detective. For the police department. I'd like to ask you some questions

Lisa What for?

Burrows We think you might be able to help us. With some . . . really, very tragic, um, crimes. Help us with some crimes that have been committed in Alabama. How old are you, ma'am?

Lisa I just turned eighteen.

Burrows Good. Can you tell me, did anyone confer with you? About legal representation?

Lisa What?

Burrows By law, you are allowed to have an attorney present here for any questioning. Did anyone explain that to you?

46

Lisa Yeah.

Burrows And do you want an attorney?

Lisa Where's my husband?

Burrows Oh, I was unaware that your husband was an attorney.

Lisa He ain't. He's a car thief.

Burrows Oh.

Lisa I was just wonderin' where he was.

Burrows He's working with some other detectives.

Lisa On what?

Burrows Just some other questions. We have for him.

Lisa Oh.

Burrows Is there anything you want to tell me about your husband?

Lisa Are you crazy?

Beat.

I mean, no.

Burrows So, do you want a lawyer?

Lisa I don't need no lawyer.

Burrows Okey dokey then, down to business. Mrs Needham, I would like to show you some photographs and have you tell me whether or not you recognize any of these people.

He pulls out three pictures and spreads them on the table in front of her. Lisa stares for a moment. She rests her elbow on the table and cups her hand over her mouth. Pointing at each one.

Now this young lady, do you recognize her?

Lisa No.

Burrows No?

Lisa No. I don't know any of them people.

Burrows What?

Lisa (*taking her hand from her mouth*) I said, 'I don't know any of them people.'

Burrows Well, that's interesting.

Lisa (*she puts her elbow back up and covers her mouth*) How come?

Burrows What about this one here, this man. Are you sure you never saw him before?

Lisa Yeah.

Burrows That's funny, 'cause he remembers you.

Lisa I don't know him.

Burrows Is there something in your hand?

Lisa What?

Burrows Are you licking something in your hand?

Lisa (*sits up, puts her hands to her side, irritated*) No.

Burrows (*very satisfied*) Well, all right then. I wonder, would you just sit back, just sit there and listen to this.

He takes out a tape and puts it in the tape recorder and presses play. A tape of Lisa's first phone call to the police is heard.

Lisa (*on tape*) 'Hello? This the police station? . . . Um, no. I don't guess it's an emergency. I just got some information –'

Burrows (*turns the sound down*) Do you recognize that?

48

Lisa (*looks at the floor*) Yes.

Burrows And what do you have to say?

Lisa (*looking up with a small smile*) Did you record that other one I made too? About them other people?

Burrows (*shocked*) Then you don't deny making the calls?

Lisa No.

Burrows Then . . . do you want to make a statement?

Lisa What do you want to know?

Burrows I want to know the truth.

Lisa (*getting to business and pointing at a picture*) Okay. This first girl, she was a girl we picked up outside the K-mart in Florence. She was runnin' away from the home, and she . . .

Burrows Wait! Stop. Let me, let me get somebody else in here, and a recorder, I mean, a court reporter, and, and a blank tape. Okay. Wait.

Lisa Okay.

> *Blackout.*
> *End of scene.*

SCENE TWO

Same as before except that a transcriber and another detective, Hugh, have joined the scene. Lisa is in mid-statement.

Lisa She was awful young, I thought, but Clint, he was happy ta have her, ya know. He was doin' stuff to her an' –

Burrows What kind of 'stuff'?

Lisa Well, like he was, you know, doin' it to her. He had her handcuffed ta the bed, and he put her on that bed, and he kinda put her at an angle before he did it to her. I think he busted somethin' in her.

Burrows So he raped her.

Lisa Yeah.

Burrows You don't care?

Lisa It wadn't nothin' new.

 Trying to explain.

He did shit like that all the time.

Burrows (*pauses. Stares at her*) Go on.

Lisa Well, the next day, he tole me I hadda kill her. He tole me how I needed ta do it and where ta take her. He give me his gun.

 Beat.

Well, I hadda go git my babies, cuz of how I was missin' 'em somethin' awful. So me and the girl, we went up ta Clint's mama's an' got my babies.

Burrows You have children?

Lisa Twins.

Burrows Where are they now?

Lisa Back up at Clint's mama's. They stay up there mostly. Clint, he don't, well, he don't like 'em much.

Burrows These are infants?

Lisa Naw. They're two and a half.

Burrows Two? And a half?

Beat. She doesn't answer.

Go on.

Lisa Anyway, me and her went up, and I got my babies, and then –

Burrows Under what pretence did you have her in the car?

Lisa I tole her I was takin' her home. She wanted to go home. So I took her up to that park, up where Clint tole me to –

Burrows Where was Clint?

Lisa Off.

Burrows Off?

Lisa Off somewhere. He was ta meet me. Later at his Mama's. So I took the girl up to the park, up where Clint said to. And then I took out the gun. I took her over to a tree and I made her sit down under it. Clint, he tole me to shoot her in the chest. But I thought, maybe I could do it somehow so that she would just fall asleep and wouldn't it hurt her none. So, I had me some needles, some hypodermic needles I got a while back, from this girl in the group home. And I had some liquid Draino. So I pulled the Draino up inta the needle and I made her sit there and I put it in her neck.

Burrows You injected Draino into her neck?

Lisa In her neck, and then in her arms, 'cause it didn't seem to be puttin' her to sleep. She just kept tellin' me it was burnin' her. It was burnin'. But it wadn't doin' nothin', I don't think. For a long time I watched her

51

but she wasn't dyin'. So then I figured Clint was right. I made her stand up and walk over ta that cliff. Then I just said, 'Turn around, look over there, look at them pretty trees,' an' I shot her in the back of the head. She just fell then, just fell off the cliff. I couldn't even see her body where she fell. She didn't cry or nothin'.

Long pause.

Burrows And, where were your babies, while you were shooting this girl?

Lisa In the back seat. Asleep.

Burrows And, um, Mrs Needham, refresh my memory. Why did you kill her?

Lisa Clint tole me to.

Burrows You do everything he tells you to do.

Lisa Yeah.

Burrows Why?

Lisa 'Cause.

Burrows Because you love him?

Lisa No sir.

Burrows Why then?

Lisa You don't want to know.

Burrows Oh, yes I do.

Lisa He'd a killed me. If I hadn't done it.

Burrows But you said he was 'off' somewhere.

Lisa Yeah.

Burrows Then why didn't you just let the girl go?

Lisa (*this idea is new to her*) I dunno. It's just that . . .
he would of known.

Burrows How?

Lisa I'm a bad liar.

Burrows Christ.

Long pause.

Hugh Why'd ya call us, Miz Needham?

Lisa (*thinks*) I hated . . . I hated ta think a' her down
there. Maybe gettin' eaten up by birds or somethin'.

Long pause.

She looked like Joanie Cunningham.

Hugh Really.

Burrows Who?

Hugh Joanie Cunningham. From *Happy Days.*

Burrows Oh. I never watched that programme.

Lisa She looked just like her.

Long pause.

Burrows Well then. That would seem to cover Kelly.
What can you tell us about Steve Culverhouse?

Lisa Who?

Burrows The young man you shot.

Lisa Oh yeah. Him. Well, I picked him and his girl-
friend up one night, off the side of the road. But I guess
he ain't dead?

Burrows No, Lisa. You left him for dead, of course, but
he managed to make it back to the road and flag down a
trucker.

Lisa His girl-friend was a retard.

Burrows What?

Lisa She was. She was a retard. But that didn't mean she wadn't nice. I guess Clint liked her okay. But then, he said I hadda kill her too.

Burrows He raped Carol Brown?

Lisa Nah. She wanted to do it. She was a retard.

Burrows I don't think she was retarded.

Lisa Oh yeah she was. That guy, he said as how he came home one night and she was playin' pin-the-tail-on-the-donkey all by herself.

Burrows (*confused*) Go back please.

Lisa That guy, her boy-friend, he tole me that. In the car.

Burrows Can you start from the beginning. From the first time you saw Steve Culverhouse and Carol Brown.

Lisa Okay.

Transcriber Excuse me.

Burrows Yes?

Transcriber Is pin-the-tail-on-the-donkey hyphenated?

Hugh Yeah. I b'lieve it is.

Transcriber Thank you.

Blackout.
End of scene.

*Same room. Steve Culverhouse sits alone, smoking a
cigarette. He turns the matchbook over and over in his
hands. Finally, a large, well-dressed man enters. He is
Carl Sheffield, Lisa's attorney. Throughout the questioning he consults notes and takes notes.*

Carl (*offering his hand*) Mr Culverhouse.

Steve (*stands. Shakes his hand*) Yessir.

Carl I'm Carl Sheffield.

Steve Yessir. I know.

Carl Thank you for coming down today.

Steve I thought I had to.

Carl I just want to ask you some questions. You understand, I'm not a policeman.

Steve Yessir. You're that girl's lawyer.

Carl That's right. I'm appointed, by the court, to defend
her.

Steve Yessir.

Carl Now, I need to hear some things from you. But you
are not required to tell me anything that would incrimi-
nate you.

Steve Nothin' would.

Carl (*smiles*) Of course not. That's just something we
say.

　Beat.

Now then. What I would like, is if you could tell me
everything you remember about that night. The twelfth.

I know this is difficult for you, but why don't you start by telling me what you and your girl-friend Carol were doing that night.

Steve We was out walkin'.

Carl To where?

Steve Nowhere. We was just out.

Sighs.

It's like I said before. I feel bad about this. But I couldn't offer Carol a lot in the way of fun. Ya know? 'Cause, we was flat busted. An' I had been at work all day and she was home. She had been in that trailer all day an' I knew she wanted ta go out an' do somethin', only I didn't have the money. So, I said, well, let's go for a walk.

Carl It was a nice evening?

Steve Yeah. We liked to walk on the road and look for nuts and bolts. Washers an' stuff. You'd be surprised how many you find. They're usually pretty rusty an' stuff, but you can clean 'em up. They're just as good as new if you clean 'em up.

Long pause.

Is that what you want to hear? Really?

Carl Yes.

Steve Well, okay. We was out walkin'. Then that girl pulled up, and she asked did we want to go for a ride. She said she had just moved here, and she was lonely. She didn't know anybody. So we said okay.

Carl Can you describe Mrs Needham's appearance to me, when you first saw her?

Steve She looked okay.

Carl Did she seem clean? Um, neat and trim?

Steve Her hair was kinda dirty.

Carl Were there any visible bruises, or scars?

Steve Not that I seen.

Carl Maybe signs of a black eye?

Steve Nah. She had circles under her eyes, maybe. Like she hadn't been sleepin'. But she seemed okay.

Beat.

Carl How long had you and Carol been living together?

Steve About eight or nine months.

Carl (*looking at his notes*) And I'm assuming she didn't work because she was retarded?

Steve She wadn't retarded.

Carl Oh. Um, maybe I'm confused, but in the police report she's listed as retarded.

Steve No way!

Carl Perhaps they're mistaken.

Steve She wadn't retarded.

Beat.

She was sweet. An' a little slow maybe. But she wadn't retarded.

Carl (*trying to explain the mistake*) Then, when you told Mrs Needham that she played pin-the-tail-on-the-donkey by herself, you weren't intending to imply that she was retarded.

Steve (*looks extremely uncomfortable*) No.

Carl You were just making conversation.

Steve I don't know.

Beat

It wadn't nothin'. I was just . . . Carol was in the back seat.

Carl Okay.

Steve She couldn't hear. She was singin' to herself.

Carl (*nods*) All right then. That's fine.

Looks at his notes.

So you and Carol had been living together for eight or nine months.

Steve Yeah.

Carl And you're currently employed at a machine shop?

Steve It's a Snapper dealership.

Carl Snapper?

Steve Lawn mowers. I fix lawn mowers.

Carl Is that interesting work?

Steve No.

Carl So Mrs Needham pulled up and she asked if you wanted to go for a ride.

Steve Yeah.

Carl Would you ride around often, with other people, or friends?

Steve No sir.

Carl But Carol would?

Steve I don't follow.

Carl (*looking at his notes again*) According to Mrs Needham, Carol told her that she would ride around, or get rides home a lot.

Steve Carol told her that? When'd she tell her that?

Carl It's something that came up in Mrs Needham's statement.

Steve What'd she say exactly?

Carl Mrs Needham related that Carol did not object to having, you know, relations with Mr Needham. That Carol would sometimes use sex as a way to get rides home.

Steve Why would she say that?

Carl It was . . . she just said that Carol said that she had never done it – I mean, had sexual intercourse with you, but that she had previously had numerous partners. I'm not sure in what context –

Steve That man raped Carol.

Carl Technically, of course –

Steve Don't mock me!

Carl Believe me, I'm not –

Steve (*with a lot of effort*) That man raped Carol. And then they took . . . they took Carol in the woods. They shot her in the back of the head. They shot her and left her there and I saw her body. They left her in a stream, mister. She was purple. Okay? She was purple. And maybe she was retarded. And what? Does that make it okay?

Carl I never meant to imply –

59

Steve Her skin was cracked open. Her skin was cracked open and she was leakin' water through her skin.

Long pause.

Carl I just have a few more questions Mr Culverhouse.

Beat. He forges ahead.

While you were in the car with Mrs Needham, did you make contact with Mr Needham?

Steve Yes.

Carl How?

Steve He came up behind us in his car and started talkin' to her on the CB.

Carl What did he say?

Steve He said, 'Hey up there. Hey. Y'all lookin' for somethin' to do?'

Carl How did he address Mrs Needham?

Steve He pretended like he didn't know her.

Carl What did he say next?

Steve He said, 'Hey. Why don't we go down ta Atlanta? Why don't we all go out and drink? Hey.' Stuff like that.

Carl And what happened?

Steve Carol wanted to go. So we said okay. Then, then that girl, she told him okay over the radio.

Carl Did Mrs Needham seem agitated at all?

Steve How?

Carl Frightened or nervous?

Steve No. She didn't seem like nothin' was wrong.

Carl What happened next?

Steve That guy said, 'Pull over here. Down that road. Then we can make some plans.' So she pulled down this dirt road a ways. Not too far. And he pulled in behind us.

Carl He was right behind you. Directly behind you?

Steve Yeah. He pulled up behind us not long after we got in her car. He pulled in behind us and got out of his car and walked up to my side of the car. I said 'hey' and he said 'hey' and we talked about maybe where we wanted to go. Then, well, I had to take a whiz, so I excused myself and got out and went in the woods a little bit.

Carl Had you been drinking?

Steve No sir, I'm a Christian.

Carl I'm sorry, I didn't know. So you went off in the woods to relieve yourself.

Steve Yeah, and then I come back out and she's standin' in the road waitin' for me with a gun.

Carl Did Mr Needham have a gun as well?

Steve None I saw.

Carl But Mrs Needham did.

Steve She had a big fuckin' gun.

Carl All right.

Steve And she told me to start walkin' down the road. I looked back and that man was down by his car with Carol. He was puttin' Carol in his car.

Carl What do you mean by 'putting her in the car'? Was he shoving her, or pushing her?

Steve No. They was just walkin'.

Beat.

You're tryin' to say it again! You're tryin' to say that she wanted to go off with him.

Carl No I'm not.

Steve Fuck you.

Carl I –

Steve I mean it! Fuck you.

Long pause.

Carl All right then. What happened next.

Steve I said, 'What are you doin'? What are you doin' with my girl-friend?' and she told me to shut up and walk down into this clearing a ways back. Then she said to stop. And then she shot me in the back.

Beat.

I fell on my face.

Carl And was there anything in Mrs Needham's behaviour, anything to make you think that what she was doing, she was doing because she was being coerced? That what she was doing, she was doing against her will?

Steve No.

Carl Well, was there anything in Mr Needham's tone or manner that seemed threatening? That seemed to imply, 'I'm in charge here. I'm in control.'

Steve Mister, if it was anything, it was just the opposite. She was into it. She was doin' just what she wanted.

Carl What makes you say that?

Steve You could tell. She was wearin' a big smile.

Carl But you said your back was to her.

Steve (*calmly*) I looked back. One time. She was smilin'. After that I could feel it.

Carl And after –

Steve I don't have anything else to say.

Carl But –

Steve (*stands*) This interview is over, mister.

Carl (*considers*) Well, then, I thank you for your time and your co-operation, Mr Culverhouse. I will be asking you more questions in court, you know.

Steve And I'll tell the judge what I'm tellin' you now. I hope they give her the chair.

Carl We'll see about that.

Steve How long you lived in Alabama?

Carl All my life.

Steve Then you know what I do. They'll give her the chair.

Carl starts to leave. Steve stops him.

Look, mister? I just want you to know, the thing was, I never even asked her to sleep with me. I never asked her 'cause I loved her.

Carl I'm sorry.

Steve Then give her the chair.

Carl She's my client.

Steve Give her the chair.

Carl I wouldn't be much of a lawyer.

Steve Give her the chair.

They stare at one another. Slow fade out.
End of scene.

SCENE FOUR

Same room. Lisa sits, fidgeting with her hair. Carl is
pacing.

Carl You've got to help me out here, Lisa.

Lisa I already told 'em I did it.

Carl I know. But maybe you didn't understand, that you
didn't have to tell the police anything. That you probably
really needed a lawyer.

Lisa I told 'em I didn't want a lawyer.

Carl I know. There's not a lot we can do about that. But
we do have something we can work with.

Lisa I don't mind bein' in jail.

Carl Lisa, we're not talking about jail. I don't think
you understand. The state is going to ask for the death
penalty. They want to give you the electric chair. They
don't care how old you are.

Lisa Oh.

Carl Right, 'Oh.' 'Oh' is right.

Pause.

Lisa But I already told 'em I did it.

Carl I know. But the thing we can work on is why you
did it.

Lisa I told 'em that too.

Carl Yes, Lisa. Just . . . just listen for a minute. Okay?

Lisa Are you mad at me?

Carl No.

Lisa Them other people askin' questions was real mad at me.

Carl Well, you killed some people, Lisa. That doesn't really make you popular.

Lisa I guess you're right.

Carl They think you killed those girls out of mean-spiritedness. Out of being mean. But I don't think that's why you did it.

Lisa You don't?

Carl No.

Lisa (*looks at him*) You ain't gonna yell at me?

Carl I rarely yell. Let's just work this out together. Now, total honesty here, why did you kill them?

Lisa I had to.

Carl Because of Clint?

Lisa Clint said I had to.

Carl You were afraid of him.

Lisa (*quietly*) Yeah.

Carl Did he hit you?

Lisa (*long pause*) Sometimes.

Carl He's a big guy.

Lisa He's mean.

Carl And you were scared of him.

Lisa nods.

But there are some difficult questions.

Lisa Like what?

Carl Like why, when Clint was miles away, you still had to kill the girl. Why didn't you let her go?

Lisa I said already.

Carl You said you're a bad liar.

Lisa I suck.

Carl Then why didn't you just leave him? You could have driven anywhere.

Lisa (*shakes her head*) I couldn't.

Carl Why not?

Lisa I don't know.

Carl That's not good enough.

Lisa Well, I don't know.

Carl (*exasperated*) Lisa!

Lisa Look – Clint found me. He found me at my mama's. He found me when they took me off ta the group home. He found me when I was in the hospital, and didn't nobody tell him where I was. He just found me. He knows how.

Carl The Department of Social Services told him where you were. You're his wife.

Long pause.

Lisa That's not what he said.

Carl So you never thought to yourself, just to let the girl go?

Lisa No. Sorry.

Carl And the same thing, with Steve Culverhouse?

Lisa Clint was right behind me. He woulda seen.

Carl He says he had already driven off with the girl. That he didn't know what you were doing.

Lisa He did?

Carl Yes.

Lisa That ain't so.

Carl Lisa, the woman that was in your hotel when the police came didn't press charges. She was on her way to Florida. Didn't want to be bothered. He'll probably plead guilty to lesser charges in exchange for his testimony and be out in a couple of years.

Lisa I don't get it.

Carl He didn't pull the trigger.

Long pause.

Lisa Well. He was there when I shot that guy, but I guess I don't got no way to prove it.

Carl And Carol? He wasn't anywhere near you and Carol.

Lisa No. Me and Carol was alone.

Carl (*slowly*) Then why?

Lisa (*quietly*) You don't understand.

Carl No Lisa. I think I do understand. But I'm not on the jury. And those are the people we have to make understand. You see?

Lisa I guess.

Carl Lisa, whether or not they believe your story is going to depend on whether or not they believe you. And you are not a convincing witness.

Lisa laughs.

See? Like that, Lisa. Like that. Why is that funny?

Lisa (*shrugs, grinning*) I dunno.

Carl You smile at all the wrong times.

Lisa (*puts her hand over her mouth*) Sorry.

Carl (*reaches over gently and lowers her hand*) Are you sorry you killed those girls?

Lisa Yes.

Carl Really?

Lisa I guess.

Carl Lisa!

Lisa They was gonna die anyway.

Carl I don't know what you mean.

Lisa There's just people as are gonna die. Just people as are gonna get killed. It's the way it is.

Carl Fate?

Lisa (*trying to explain*) No. They got in the car with me.

Carl That's why you killed them?

Lisa No. That's why they died.

Beat. She tries a new tack.

Now you, would you of ever got in the car with me?

Carl No.

Lisa See? They did. Because they're of that type. It's just a thing that happens to a type. And it woulda kept happenin' forever.

Long pause.

Carl That's why you called the police.

Lisa No.

Carl Yes, Lisa. Yes it is.

Lisa I don't know why I called the police.

Carl Don't tell the jury that. Tell the jury that you called to stop it. You were frightened to death and you would rather be in jail than out there again with Clint.

Lisa But I wadn't thinkin' that.

Carl I don't care. You say it.

Lisa It won't work.

Carl It won't work if you don't make it work.

Lisa You tell 'em what you want but they ain't gonna believe it. They'll know just by lookin' at me. They'll know that it never even occurred to me that I didn't hafta do it.

Carl It really didn't?

Lisa No.

Pause.

Carl Where's your little piano?

Lisa Who told you that?

Carl Detective Burrows. He said you held on to it like crazy.

Lisa So.

Carl He said your daddy gave it to you.

Lisa So.

Carl That it was all you took with you when you left home. At fifteen.

Lisa I took all my clothes.

Carl That's not the point.

Lisa (*shakes her head*) Go on then, say what you want.

Carl It's not just me, though, Lisa. It's what you say too.

Lisa I ain't gonna say that crap.

Carl Do you want to die? Is that it?

Lisa It doesn't matter.

Carl It does!

Lisa It doesn't! You tell me one way that it matters.

Carl It matters a lot.

Lisa No it don't. That girl I killed, and them two other people, if I hadn't called the police, if that guy hadn't of lived, wouldn't anybody even know they was gone.

Carl I'm sure somebody –

Lisa No you ain't. You ain't sure.

Beat.

Carl Well, I suppose it's possible . . .

Lisa It's more than 'possible'. It's the goddamn truth.

Pause.

Carl Now that's precisely the sort of thing you should not say in the courtroom.

Lisa stares at him. Lights fade out.
End of scene.

SCENE FIVE

A trailer on the grounds of the prison. It looks amazingly like the old motel rooms they used to live in, except even more bare. There are no chairs. There is one bed, relatively neatly made up with an old bedspread and pillows. The door opens and Clint enters. He is cleaned up a bit, wearing a clean t-shirt and jeans. A voice from off says, 'Wait there.'

Clint Okay.

He looks around for a place to sit, sees only the bed, and sits down carefully, perched on the edge.
Almost right away, Lisa enters, wearing jeans, a work shirt, and flip flops.
The guard sticks his head in.

Guard Okay. You two got thirty minutes. At twenty-five minutes, I give a warnin' knock on the door. Then at thirty, I open it. There are no surveillance cameras in the trailer. Got it?

Clint Yessir. Thank you.

Guard You got a watch?

Clint Yessir.

Guard Watch the time then. You don't want no surprises.

He closes the door.

Clint Yessir.

He looks at his watch.

Okay.

Lisa Hey.

Clint Oh hey, honey!

Laughs

C'mere and gimme a hug.

She goes to him. They hug awkwardly.

Here, sit down.

He pats the bed.

Lisa I don't mind standin'.

Clint Okay, okay. Hey. You look great.

Lisa Thanks.

Clint I like them sandals.

Lisa Thanks.

Pause.

Clint This is kinda weird, ain't it?

Lisa Yeah.

Clint You sure you don't wanta sit down? Just ta get off your feet? I mean, there ain't no chairs.

Lisa Okay then.

She sits on the bed. He sits down beside her.

How are you then?

Clint Oh, hell honey, I'm fine. When hadn't I been fine?

Lisa Never I guess.

Pause.

Clint Look honey, we don't, we don't gotta do nothin' here. I'm just so happy to see you and talk to you and be able to touch you even. Would it be okay if we just sat here and I held your hand?

Lisa I guess so.

She doesn't offer her hand. Clint takes it.

Clint Lisa honey, I gotta start out by sayin' one thing.

Lisa What's that?

Clint I am so sorry.

Lisa It ain't your fault.

Clint It is too my fault! Shit honey, wouldn't none of this mess happened if it wadn't for me.

Lisa You didn't kill nobody.

Clint In a way I did.

Lisa How?

Clint I give you the gun, didn't I? And in a way, I guess I give you the motivation.

Lisa You mean, motivation, like sayin', 'Go kill that girl.' You mean like that?

Clint (*pauses*) Now Lisa. I unnerstand, how you had to say things in court. Ugly things like that. I understand all them lawyers, they had you sayin' things just so you could not look so bad. But honey, this is you and me sittin' here. Clint and Lisa and nobody else. Now you can say the truth ta me.

73

Pause.

You didn't really mean all that stuff did ya?

Lisa How do you know what I said in there?

Clint I read it in the paper honey. Every mornin' they'd bring me the paper and say, 'Hey Clint! Look what your wife's sayin' today. Your wife's sayin' you're the baddest thing since King Kong, man.'

Lisa They brung you a paper to your cell?

Clint Yeah.

Lisa In here we only got one room we can read the paper in. I only get to go down there one time week.

Clint That's too bad.

Lisa And here, we don't get outta jail after eighteen months. Are you glad ta be outta jail?

Clint Well, yeah, I'm glad. Only, I'm sorry I was ever in it 'cause it meant I couldn't come and help you. I couldn't be there for you.

Lisa That's okay.

Clint No it ain't honey! Jesus. Girl, listen ta me. This is the worse thing that ever happened to you and now you got ta sit in here and face it all by yourself and I feel terrible about that. I feel terrible. I just want to love you and make you feel better. That's all.

Lisa (*quietly*) Okay then. I feel better.

Clint You do?

Lisa Yeah I do.

Clint An' you didn't mean none of that stuff you said about me? Tell me that.

74

Lisa I didn't mean it.

Clint Okay then. You did what was right honey. Don't feel bad. You were just tryin' ta protect yourself, 'cause wadn't nobody there to do it for you.

Lisa That's right.

Clint Okay.

Beat

That's settled then.

Pause.

So what else is new?

Lisa Nothin' really.

Clint What about the appeal? Your lawyer's got a appeal goin', right?

Lisa I guess so. Yeah.

Clint How's it goin?

Lisa Okay, I guess.

Clint Good, good.

Hugs her suddenly.

Aw honey! It's so good ta see you.

Lisa (*into his chest*) It's good ta see you too, Clint.

Starts to reach down to her pocket.

I wanta give you somethin'.

Clint (*delighted*) Oh yeah?

Lisa Yeah.

Clint What is it?

Lisa (*digs in her pocket. Pulls out a dollar*) Here.

Clint A dollar?

Lisa It's all the money I got but you can take it.

Clint What do I need a dollar for honey?

Lisa I just wanted to give you somethin'. I gotta go now.

She stands up quickly, crosses to the door.

Clint What?

He follows her.

Lisa (*starts knocking on the door*) I gotta go.

Shouts

Hey! Hey!

Clint (*takes her arm*) It ain't time yet.

Looks at his watch, thinks.

It ain't even half time yet.

Lisa (*shouting*) Open the door!

Clint Why don't you wanta stay?

Lisa I got a lot to do.

Shouts and pounds with her free hand.

Open the goddamn door!

The door opens suddenly.

Guard What is it?

Lisa I wanta go now.

Guard Your time's not up.

Lisa I wanta go back to my cell now, please.

Guard Is there a problem?

Lisa No, he's just faster than most.

She steps out past him.

Guard (*only slightly puzzled*) Okay then.

Turns his back to Clint, blocking the door. Yells.

Walt?

Beat

Come get Mrs Needham. She wants to go back.

Turns back to Clint.

Okay Mr Needham. I'll escort you back as soon as your wife's cleared the yard.

Clint Can't I just talk to her?

Guard No sir.

Clint (*yells over the guard's shoulder*) Lisa? What'd I do?

Lisa (*off. Yells back, retreating*) Bye, Clint!

Clint (*yells again*) How come you're mad?

Beat. No answer.

Lisa! They took the babies! They put 'em in a foster home!

No answer.

Goddamn it!

Guard Sometimes they turn in here. I seen it happen more than once. They lose their taste for men.

Clint (*stares at him a moment*) Fuck you.

Guard (*shrugs*) Sometimes it happens is all. It's natural.

Clint She ain't never loved nobody but me, mister. Nobody but me.

Guard I'm just sayin'.

Clint You don't know shit.

They stand. Blackout.
End of scene.

SCENE SIX

Prison visiting room. Carl is waiting, reading over some papers. He seems tired. The guard enters, followed by Lisa, carrying her toy piano.

Guard Here she is.

Carl Thanks.

Guard exits.

Lisa.

Lisa Hey.

Carl I see you have your piano.

Lisa Yeah.

Carl Shall we?

He gestures toward the chair.

Lisa Okay.

She sits.

Carl I filed for the appeal. I don't have any real sense of what will happen, though, to be honest. The review usually takes quite a while.

Beat.

I say 'usually' but I don't really know. I've never represented anybody on death row. But I think, at any rate, that our time is best spent now in going back over the details, back over your testimony, and getting it right. In the event that we're granted another trial.

Lisa I'm sorry I made you so mad.

Carl You didn't make me mad.

Lisa I know I didn't do good.

Carl I don't know why you say that.

Lisa 'Cause I lost.

Carl Well, I'm sorry not to have won for you. I think that some of my tactics may have . . . alienated the jury.

Lisa (*laughs*) You pissed 'em off.

Carl Yes. Well.

Lisa Half of them guys beat the shit outta their wives. And them wives, they say, 'Shit, I git beat up, I don't go killin' nobody over it.'

Carl You could be right.

Lisa It's okay. I wish you wouldn't feel bad.

Carl For Christ's sake, Lisa! You're going to the electric chair.

Lisa I still wish you wouldn't feel bad. It ain't your fault.

Carl I just . . . let me feel bad, if I want to feel bad.

Pause.

Are you getting everything you need here?

Lisa I guess. I did like it better before I lost. I don't get to see nobody else now. I gotta eat by myself.

Carl You liked being around other prisoners?

Lisa They wadn't all bad.

Carl Well, I'm sorry you had so much time to get to know them.

Lisa But this ain't so bad. I got my own room. And they let me go outside every day.

Carl That's good.

Hands her an envelope.

These are the transcripts of your testimony. I want you to start by reading back over what you said, and seeing if there's anything you left out, that you can remember now.

Lisa How long before they kill me?

Carl What?

Lisa How long?

Carl But what about the appeal?

Lisa Yeah, but after that.

Carl I'm hoping to reverse the judge's decision.

Lisa Okay, but after that.

Carl (*sighs*) Well, there's only one other prisoner here on death row, and it's been ten years since she was convicted.

Lisa (*quietly pleased*) Wow.

Carl (*shaking his head*) I can't even begin to understand you.

Lisa Yeah. But I appreciate that you try.

Long pause. Carl stares at her. He looks as if he might cry. He looks down at his notes. Beat.

Carl (*quietly*) Do you mind if we talk about this later? I'm more tired than I thought.

Lisa Okay.

He starts to get his things together. She pushes the piano towards him.

Here.

Carl What?

Lisa It's all I got, an' I want to give it to you.

Carl I can't take this.

Lisa Yes you can.

She pushes it in front of him.

I wish it wadn't busted.

Carl This is too precious to you. I can't.

Lisa But all the keys still work. See?

She plinks a couple of keys. Carl studies her.

Go on. Take it.

Pause. He stares at it.

Look, I want to give it to you.

Small beat. Conceding something, to get him to take it.

It's like you said. It's important to me.

Carl looks at her, then at the piano, then slowly, he taps out the opening to 'Mary Had a Little Lamb,' on it.

Hey! That's good! I couldn't never play nothin' on it.

Carl Anybody can play that.

Lisa Not me.

Carl Really?

Lisa Daddy just give it to me. He didn't show me how it worked.

Carl That's a shame.

Standing.

It is. Come around here.

She hesitates.

Come on. I'll show you.

Lisa Okay I guess.

She gets up, comes around the table.

Carl Okay. Now, sit down.

She sits.

Now, this is not a full keyboard, obviously. But here, you have your white keys, and your black keys. Each key is a note, and each note has a name. Here. See this? This is the key to know. This is the middle C.

Lisa (*tapping it*) Middle C.

Carl (*tapping*) Up two to E.

Lisa (*tapping slowly*) C, D, E.

Carl Good. Now watch.

Taps out the first notes of the song, just up to the point where it skips to G, and stops.

Try that far.

Lisa (*to herself, picking out the tune and naming the notes. Carl helps her out along the way*) E D C D, E E E,

D D D, E. (*Looks up, smiling.*) Hey!

Carl (*points*) Now G twice.

> *Lisa reaches out, taps G twice.*

Okay. Now, back to the beginning. E, D, C, D, E E E . . .

> *Lisa plays it.*

One more E.

> *She plays it. Carl reaches over her shoulder, finishes the song, playing and singing.*

'Whose fleece was white as snow.'

Lisa (*mimics him, playing and singing*) 'Whose fleece was white as snow.'

Carl Right, back to middle C.

Lisa (*taps the middle C again, looks at the piano, looks up*) Teach me another one.

Carl Okay.

> *Pulling a chair up next to hers.*

Move over.

> *He takes the piano.*

Now pay attention.

> *He starts to play 'Jingle Bells.'*
> *Lisa watches.*
> *Slow fade out.*
> *End of play.*